HARLOW'S

PONIES

This book belongs to

....

HARLOW'S
PONIES
Contents

34 **Super summer**
My favourite time of
year!

36 **Popcorn does...**
Showjumping!

40 **Half hour riding
hacks..**
Flatwork!

42 **Why I love...**
Welshes!

44 **Picture perfect**
Get amazing pics of
your pony

48 **Pony puzzles**
Test your knowledge!

50 **Cloudy does...**
Hacking!

54 **Out and about**
My top four fave horsey
days out

56 **Make a horsey
candle**
The cutest addition to
your bedroom

58 **Care guide:
mucking out**
Tidy up your pony's
stable

60 **Why I love...**
Shetlands!

62 **Trailer tour**
Take a look around

64 **Fan-tastic!**
Are you a mega fan?

6 **Splendid spring**
It's such a stunning
season!

8 **Panda does...**
Dressage!

12 **Half hour riding
hacks...**
Hacking!

14 **Simply the best**
Why ponies are great

16 **Happy holidays**
My four fave horsey
adventures

20 **Why I love...**
Dartmoors!

22 **Care guide: feeding**
An essential part of
pony care

24 **The White Family**
Horsey time is family
time

28 **Meet Panda**
Get to know our
newest addition

30 **Make a stable
birthday card**
For your best
pony pal

32 **My YouTube
journey**
Our story so far

66   Awesome autumn
The season of colour!

68   Rolo does...
Showing!

74   Day in the life
Find out what the ponies get up to!

76   Half hour riding hacks...
Jumping!

78   At the movies
Make incredible videos of your pony

80   Make crunchy horseshoes
A yummy snack!

82   Meet Rolo
Get to know our showing superstar

84   Why I love...
Connies!

86   Popcorn does...
Cross-country!

92   Care guide: tack cleaning
Keep yours in top condition!

94   Pick of the bunch
Which of my ponies are you most like?

98   Wonderful winter
It's such a pretty season!

100   Behind the scenes
Making the 2024 yearbook!

HARLOW'S PONIES

Published by DJ Murphy (Publishers) Ltd, Olive Studio, Grange Road, Tilford, Farnham, Surrey GU10 2DQ

Who did what in Harlow Yearbook 2024
Harlow Luna White
Contributors Sarah Burgess, Halima Crabtree, Louise Kittle, Nicky Moffatt, Megan Xavier-Witherington
Design Sarah Garland
Photography Peter Nixon, Chelsea White, First Class Images
Managing Director Zoe Cannon
Commercial Director Abi Cannon

Harlow Yearbook is produced under license by DJ Murphy (Publishers) Ltd.
© Copyright DJ Murphy (Publishers) Ltd.

Printed in Italy by Rotolito S.p.A.

ISBN 978-1-913787-19-6

MIX
Paper from responsible sources
FSC® C005461

RRP £12.99

SPLENDID SPRING

Clock changes and post-school rides can only mean one thing – spring is here!

Like every equestrian, I get so excited when spring comes around because it means lighter evenings and snippets of sunshine. My ponies absolutely love spring, too – after all, the countryside bursts into life and everything turns greener!

RIDING

Back on track ☐

With the competition season approaching and the ground improving, it's the ideal time of year to boost my ponies' fitness, and going to the gallops is sooo much fun! I like to set out some goals and make a plan to get the boys back into full work mode and ready for all the amazing adventures ahead of us.

Cross-country's calling ☐

Arena XC during the winter is pretty sweet, but being out in an open, grassy field where you can go for a good gallop between fences is even sweeter. Putting all of our XC-riding skills to the test when schooling shows me just how far I've come and how much my ponies have improved over the winter.

CARE

No more fluff ☐

It's my absolute fave thing when Popcorn's coat turns golden again! Nothing beats seeing his soft, shiny summer coat come through and I always groom him loads to help him through the moulting process – I'll do anything to speed up the golden-boy transition!

Diet decisions ☐

The extra grass growth and more turnout time in spring means the ponies are at risk of becoming overweight. To keep the boys healthy and trim, I make sure they have a good exercise routine, weightape them regularly and slowly reduce the amount of hard feed they get – they definitely don't need the extra cals that they have to have in the winter.

PANDA DOES...

DRESSAGE

Learning all the different dressage moves is so much fun, and Panda's a bit of a dressage pro

I'm excited about competing Panda in dressage competitions this year. I know I'm biased but I think he's a real head turner.

With his lovely way of going and smart paces, I'm hoping to impress the judges and gain good marks. Let's take a closer look at this discipline.

What is dressage?

A bit like gymnastics for horses, dressage competitions involve riding lots of movements under the watchful eye of a judge. There are 11 different levels, ranging from Intro, which is done in walk and trot, to Grand Prix, where top riders perform tricky movements like piaffe, passage and pirouettes.

What's involved?

Thinking of having a go? Why not start by trying an Intro or a Preliminary level test? At the lower levels you'll be asked to show turns and circles, serpentines, straight centre lines and tons of transitions.

Accuracy is the key, so if you want to earn higher marks, it's really important you carry out the movements exactly where and when your test sheet asks you to do them.

If you've never competed in dressage competitions before, it's worth booking some lessons with a dressage instructor. They'll be able to tell you exactly what's involved and talk you through the way you should be riding each movement.

PANDA'S PROPOSAL

Did you know that you won't be marked on how well turned out your pony is and you don't have to plait for dressage? However, if you look smart you'll feel way more confident, too. Plus, making an effort to look your best creates a more professional appearance. Win, win!

WHAT TO WEAR

If a competition is run under British Dressage rules, you'll need to wear...

PONY

- snaffle bridle (at the lower levels). Read the rule book to see which bits and nosebands are permitted ☐
- correctly fitted saddle with stirrups and girth ☐
- plain saddle pad ☐

RIDER

- correctly fitted helmet that meets current safety standards ☐
- hairnet or hairband ☐
- competition shirt ☐
- black, blue or tweed jacket ☐
- stock or tie with tie pin ☐
- white or beige jods ☐
- long or short boots ☐
- gloves ☐

PANDA'S PROPOSAL

Us ponies can pick up on our riders' feelings, so if nerves are getting the better of you remember to take a lots of deep breaths. You could also have a go at some online dressage to build your confidence. This is when you film your test at home, upload it to a website and get marked like a real test!

Perfect prep

Here's my plan of action to get you and your pony dressage ready this year...

1. Decide what level you want to compete at, then order the test sheets so you can learn the movements.
2. Book some lessons with your instructor, who will

I wear boots while warming up, but Harlow has to remove them before we enter the competition arena. This is because they're not allowed in actual tests.

be able to give you advice on how to gain higher marks.
3. Practise the movements in your test in between lessons.
4. Watch a few competitions before entering one.
5. Look up local dressage events in your area then send off your entries! Good luck!

Half-hour RIDING HACKS!

HACKING

Turn your hacks into productive schooling sessions with my quick guide!

I love riding through the gorgeous countryside but I don't always have time to go hacking, so I try to incorporate some dressage moves along my route to get the best of both worlds. Here's my half-hour hacking plan...

Starting out

10 min

I'm lucky enough to have access to lots of off-road hacking, so as I head out towards the fields and bridleways, I ask Rolo for a couple of halt transitions in between encouraging him to walk on really positively. As he warms up, I slowly ask him to work in an outline and progress to trot-walk-trot transitions to help keep him focused and to check he's listening to my aids.

Stepping up

10 min

Like most ponies, Rolo feels more active and responsive when hacking and I always take advantage of his higher energy levels to help boost our flatwork skills. For my first exercise, I ask him to step sideways and forwards across the path we're riding on, first in walk, then we'll have a go in trot. We practise moving from one side to the other and back again – it's a good test of his suppleness and straightness.

5 min

Next level

Towards the end of our hack, I find a stretch of grass to have a go at some walk to canter transitions. It's the perfect time to practise this fun movement when Rolo's feeling more alert, and it gives me the chance to polish my aids, too.

5 min

That's a wrap!

It's cool-down time for the final five minutes of my speedy hack while we make our way back to the yard. I lengthen my reins to let Rolo stretch his head and neck down and give him a scratch on his wither to tell him he's been a good boy!

HEARD IT FROM HARLOW

Wearing high-vis when hacking is sooo important, whether you go hacking on the roads or through open fields! It helps to keep you and your pony safe and visible to others.

SIMPLY THE BEST

What do you love the most about ponies?

There is absolutely no doubt that ponies are my favourite animals – there's just so much to love about these amazing, and adorable, creatures! Here are my four fave things...

Big pats for the super-talented Panda!

Kind and caring

Whether there's something super-exciting to celebrate or you've had a day at school that you'd rather forget, ponies are always there for us when we need them most. They take us for who we are and don't judge our thoughts and feelings. They make great listeners and give the very best cuddles. Plus there's no better feeling than when you realise your confidence has reached new heights thanks to your pony.

Best of friends

Not only do ponies make fab friends themselves, they also give us the chance to find like-minded pals! Riding schools and livery yards are full of pony-mad people and you're sure to find a BFF who you can enjoy going on epic horsey adventures with.

Tons of talents

Ponies have sooo many super-cool skills. From jumping big fences to trotting sideways across the arena, they're such talented animals and we're so lucky to be able to ride and enjoy them! Some ponies, like Popcorn, can even do party tricks – it's totally hilarious, and so clever of him when he smiles on command!

My ponies mean the world to me and give me so much love, so I always make time to give some back to them! They love pamper sessions, munching on tasty treats and extra time in the field with their friends!

Cantering with the golden boy!

Endless adventures

You'll never be short on amazing memories when ponies are involved and there are millions of fun things to do with your four-legged friends. Galloping pocket-sized ponies along the seashore, exploring the local countryside and stopping off for picnics and learning new disciplines and skills you never thought you'd be capable of – these are just some of the incredible adventures that ponies bring into our lives.

HAPPY HOLIDAYS

Find out my top four favourite horsey holidays!

I've been lucky enough to go to so many amazing places all over the world and every time I travel with my family, we can't resist involving ponies somehow! From beach rides in Dubai to skiing with horses in France, these are my four best horsey hols so far.

HEARD IT FROM HARLOW

If you're going on holiday with your family, why not do some research beforehand to find a few horsey activities? There will definitely be things you can do – even if your family isn't super horsey!

Avoriaz, France

I went with my mum and we had the most magical Christmas Day skijoring when we were in France! It was actually really tough and much harder than it looks, but it was sooo cool. The ponies were very powerful and the views were beautiful! It's definitely the most unusual horsey sport I've ever experienced and I'd love to do it again!

California, USA

Our trip to the USA wasn't exactly a horsey holiday, but we were very excited to go to an American tack shop for the first time! It was so cool to see all the items we don't have here in England and, of course, we had to get the ponies some tasty snacks! We also bought a lot more than we'd intended – oops!

Doha, Qatar

The Al Shaqab Equestrian Centre was horsey heaven. The facilities were absolutely incredible – it didn't seem real! The centre has more than 750 horses and even a barn for miniature ponies! I was also lucky enough to have a showjumping lesson and course walk with Edwina Tops while in Qatar, which was really interesting and I learnt masses!

Dubai, UAE

Swimming with horses at sunset in Dubai was literally idyllic and one of my best memories. The skyline was amazing and the whole experience was even better than I'd imagined! I also went on a desert ride – galloping through the dunes was a dream come true! The horse I rode was so calm and careful, I could literally just enjoy the ride!

"Popcorn is literally the most perfect pony in the world – just look at that face!"

Why I LOVE Dartmoors

Dartmoors are so fab, with their flashy paces and cute, friendly faces

Ace all-rounder

Dartmoors make fantastic first ponies because of their lovely temperaments, and they're also so talented! They can strut their stuff in the show ring, flick their toes during dressage and fly high in the showjumping arena.

Tough stuff

Sure-footed, strong and sturdy, the conformation of Dartmoor ponies makes them so tough – they're like little pocket rockets!

Hair goals

Their long flowing manes are so iconic and totally make Dartmoors stand out from the crowd. Did you know Dartmoors' manes should be left natural for showing? Their manes evolved to be really thick to help keep the ponies warm in the wild!

Block print

Pure-bred Dartmoors should have a single coat colour and almost no white markings – coloured ponies can't be registered with the breed's society. They're most commonly bay, black, brown or chestnut – so gorgeous!

In the wild

There are still feral Dartmoor ponies living on the moors and if you visit the area, you'll get to see them in their natural habitat. Isn't that amazing?

THE LOWDOWN

Did you know the Dartmoor breed originated in Devon in southwest England? It's believed they've been living on the moors of Dartmoor for thousands of years – how cool is that?

Rolo's round-up

Dartmoor ponies like me are often bred for the show ring! You'll often find Dartmoors competing in many classes, from mountain-and-moorland and first-ridden, all the way to lead-rein classes.

CARE
guide:
FEEDING

Learn how to feed a pony with my handy guide

Ponies love being in the field and eating grass, but if they're stabled, they need other kinds of food, such as hay, to fulfil their energy needs. Here's my easy guide to feeding a pony before bedtime...

HEARD IT FROM HARLOW

Popcorn's been poorly with stomach ulcers before, so I make sure he gets some hay or a handful of feed to line his tummy before I ride, as this helps to prevent the ulcers from coming back.

Popcorn having a pre-ride munch!

1. Before getting started, speak to your yard manager and a nutritionist for advice on what type of hard feed, if any, your pony needs. When you're ready to make up his feed, place your pony's feed bowl on the floor and, using a scoop, add the recommended amount of feed.

2. Some ponies need supplements to help keep them healthy and support any problems they have, such as poor hoof quality. If you've been advised to give your pony a supplement, measure out the amount he needs and add it to his feed. Then, add some water and give it a good mix!

3. The feed is now ready for your pony, and he'll be so excited when he sees you coming with his dinner! Whether he's in his stable or tied up on the yard, pop the bowl on the floor in front of him and let him enjoy his tasty meal! Be sure to give the feed room a sweep and quick tidy up, too.

~ THE LOWDOWN ~

It's important ponies are fed lots of fibre, little and often, because that's how their guts have evolved to work. They need an almost constant supply of food to help keep them healthy and should never go more than eight hours without eating.

Equi-vation

4. While your pony's enjoying his hard feed, you can make his haynet for the night. Head over to the barn where you store his hay and grab a haynet. Then, hook it onto something, or ask a friend to hold it open – this will make it sooo much easier for you to fill up.

5. Ponies need around 1.5% of their bodyweight per day in forage, so ask your yard manager to help you work out how much he needs. Fill up his haynet and weigh it to check you're not feeding too much or too little – take some out or add a bit more if you need to!

6. It's best for ponies to eat their hay from the floor – that's how they graze naturally and it's better for their breathing. So, I tip the haynet out onto the stable floor in a neat pile. But if your pony is greedy or extra messy and needs his hay in a haynet, ask an adult to show you how to tie it up safely!

The White family

The ponies are such a huge part of our family and help us make the most special memories

Spending time with my family is so important to me and when it involves the ponies, its makes our time together even more special. The White family's schedule is definitely full on, but we never take for granted the time we have together!

HEARD IT FROM HARLOW

Due to my mum's job as a photographer we get to travel all over the world to the most incredible places! Our best trip yet has got to be the Maldives – the villa we stayed in was amazing!

Following in my footsteps

Harlen has improved so much in such a short space of time and I couldn't be more proud of him! He's officially taken over Cloudy's reins now and I can't wait to see what they achieve!

Harlen has improved so much in such a short space of time!

Mini me

Me and my mum are so close and I couldn't love her more – she does so much for me and I wouldn't have achieved half of the things I have without her!

Now we have Panda, we – me, Mum and Harlen – can go on riding adventures together, which will be amazing – and probably a bit hectic!

Summer is the White family's fave season! When the days are longer and we're on summer holidays, it means we can spend loads more time together – the dream!

Harlow's riding school

My auntie isn't horsey, but my cousins absolutely adore the ponies and love coming for a ride! Cloudy is the perfect size for them and we have hours of fun and giggles trotting around the arena and going for hacks all over the farm.

Quality time

My cousin, Lexi, is one of my best friends and she's amazing! She loves sleeping over at our house, then coming to shows and helping with the ponies – she grooms, tacks up and even takes pics and videos for me. This means my mum can focus on getting vlog content and Lexi can get the perfect snaps for my Insta!

HEARD IT FROM HARLOW

My nanny and grandad are literally our heroes. From organising our packed lunches to helping us tidy up after a long day, they're the best and sooo supportive!

Insider info

If he's not riding Cloudy, you'll often find Harlen whizzing around the farm in his super-speedy buggy!

Meet Panda

FACT FILE

- **DATE OF BIRTH**
  3 May 2015
- **HEIGHT**
  14.2hh
- **BREED**
  Connemara
- **BEST EQUINE FRIEND**
  Rolo
- **FAVE TREAT**
  Anything!
- **FAVE ACTIVITY**
  Dressage and hacking!
- **BEST COLOUR**
  Baby blue

As the newest member of the White family, Panda was thrown straight into the spotlight and, boy, did he wow us all!

Although tricky to keep clean, he's the perfect model and we quickly discovered that he can turn his hoof to anything. He's awesome on the XC course and excels at dressage – we even won our first comp! I can't wait to see what the future holds for us – watch this space!

Bear hug

Panda has that classic Connie character! He's cool, calm and collected – oh and cute, obviously! It's actually crazy how chilled out he is. Wherever we go, he just takes it all in his stride and focuses on his job!

He's sooo cuddly, too, and has the weirdest scratchy spot – it's between his front legs. How random is that! Panda loves being pampered and having scratchies in the sunshine!

Insider info

Panda loves smiling for absolutely no reason at all! I find it hilarious and so cute!

He just takes it all in his stride and focuses on his job!

HEARD IT FROM HARLOW

My goals with Panda are to climb the levels in dressage, do some eventing and maybe even go to Horse of the Year Show one day to do some showing! He's so talented and I'm very determined!

MAKE STABLE BIRTHDAY CARD

Five steps to creating the best birthday card ever!

Whether it's your pony's, friend's or a family member's birthday, why not make them this adorable personalised birthday card? It's super-easy and you can make it unique! Here's how...

Let's go

Kit check

- black felt-tip pen
- pony template
- A4 brown card
- wool or ribbon
- black and coloured card, including colours to match your pony

1 Fold the brown card in half and on one side draw an 8cm x 11cm rectangle in the middle of the top half. Ask an adult to help you cut it out.

2 On a piece of black card, cut out two semi-circles and a small rectangle for the hinges and door handle.

3 Download the pony shape template from **bit.ly/STABLE_CARD**. Print the body template onto card that's the same colour as your pony's body, and the mane, tail and face markings template onto another piece of coloured card. Cut out the shapes and stick them in onto the brown card so the pony's head is visible through the window.

4 Cut out 13 small triangles from your coloured card and spell out happy birthday. Stick them and the wool onto the front of your card to make bunting.

5 Write a message inside the card and ta-dah! An adorable personalised pony birthday card for someone special!

HEARD IT FROM HARLOW

Why not decorate your stable card for another occasion? You could cut out a stocking and hang it on the door to create a Christmas card, or cover it in pink hearts for someone special on Valentine's Day!

MY ♥ YOUTUBE

7.1 million views

Where it all began

I was only five in my first horsey video! I did a grooming tutorial with a Shetland called Teddy and it's had sooo many views!

FIRST PONY!

FIRST 2 WEEKS OWNING POPCORN!

221k views

Popcorn joined the family

After a long break from riding, Popcorn came into our lives in March 2021 and we've never looked back!

IT'S SHOW TIME!

228k views

Harlen's first show

I was so proud watching Harlen at his first ever show and I can't wait to see what he gets up to with Cloudy in the future!

NEW PONY!

677k views

Rolo kicked off my showing career

The gorgeous Rolo came home at the end of 2022 and really showed me what showing is all about!

JOURNEY

It's been a crazy ride so far and there's still so much more to come!

Our first ever show

We started getting out and about more with Popcorn. Our first show was a whirlwind and we've come such a long way since then!

My racing journey began

Cloudy joined our family in 2022 and we had an amazing year racing together! Riding at Badminton was definitely the highlight!

Horsey adventures abroad

Along the way we've travelled around the world and experienced so many incredible equestrian adventures!

Starting @harlowplays

I absolutely love playing horsey games when I'm not at the yard, and now I get to share all my gaming tips with you on my channel!

SUPER SUMMER

From gleaming coats to dreamy sunset rides, there's so much to love about summer!

I ce cream stops while hacking, days out in the sunshine and pamper sessions for the ponies, summer is definitely my favourite season. My boys get lots of turnout time in summer so I'm sure it's their fave, too!

RIDING

Endless fun ☐

The long summer days mean there's sooo much time for horsey adventures. Whether it's going for a hack on the beach, having lessons on all the ponies or spending the day at a horsey event watching pro riders – there's always something to learn and improve on and what better time to do it than summer?

It's show time ☐

I compete all year round but summer show days are the best. Whatever discipline I'm doing I always have the best time and so much fun. Working towards my goals is important for progressing my riding skills, but getting out and about as much as I can is so good for the ponies' confidence, and mine too!

CARE

Feeling spacey ☐

Summer means sunshine and higher temps, so it's time to say goodbye to winter rugs (cleaning and storing them away correctly), and hello to fly rugs, masks and sprays! I like to keep my ponies fully protected from the pesky bugs, so they channel their inner aliens when spending time in the field during the summer – they look hilarious!

Scrub up ☐

When the weather's warm I love to give the ponies a good clean-up and make them shine from head to toe! Starting with a bath and finishing off with a spritz of coat shine and a dollop of hoof balm, they all look so handsome after a pamper session. Bathing too often can lead to skin and coat problems, so I do it once a fortnight to help keep their skins and coats in top condition.

POPCORN DOES...

SHOWJUMPING

Want to take the jumping world by storm? I'm riding Popcorn and we'll help you do just that!

Showjumping is a really popular sport and as well as pure showjumping competitions, it's also a phase in eventing.

It's great fun, so why not book some lessons and give it a go? You never know, you could even be the next Sienna Charles!

What is showjumping?

A course of coloured and rustic fences in an arena or a grass ring.

What's involved?

The aim is to jump around the course without knocking poles or having any refusals or run-outs. Then, you'll go into a jump-off when you'll be timed against the clock. The fastest clear round in the jump-off wins the class!

Courses are made up of lots of different fences, including uprights and spreads, although and you might find two fences close together in a combination.

You can walk the course before the class starts. This is important to help you learn the route and work out the best line to ride between each of the fences.

POPCORN'S POINTERS

Jumping's easier for ponies when we have a canter with plenty of energy. Next time you ride, see how active you can get your pony's canter, then count the three-beat rhythm of the canter in your head, trying to keep it the same. Then try to do it over poles and jumps!

HEARD IT FROM HARLOW

Your position over fences makes a big difference to your pony, so remember to work on your balance. I like to practise standing up in my stirrups and walking, trotting and cantering around the arena in a light seat. It's harder than it sounds!

WHAT TO WEAR

Any colour goes when jumping at home, but for competition you'll need...

PONY
- correctly fitted saddle with a girth, saddlepad and stirrups ☐
- bridle with a bit and noseband that are competition legal and offer you full control ☐
- boots to protect your pony's legs ☐

RIDER
- correctly fitted helmet ☐
- black, blue or tweed jacket ☐
- show shirt ☐
- beige or white jods ☐
- Long boots or short ones with gaiters ☐

POPCORN'S POINTERS

Showjumping ponies need to be really supple, and gridwork can help. It's basically a line of at least three fences in a row. Why not ask your instructor if you can try some in your next lesson so you can see the results for yourself?

Perfect prep

Want to be really good at showjumping? Then try out some of my top tips...
- book some lessons with your instructor so you can work on your own and your pony's skills
- keep your pony supple and strong by doing regular flatwork sessions

Showjumping's great fun, so why not book some lessons and give it a go?

POPCORN'S POINTERS

A good exercise you can try is to use V-poles like Harlow and I are doing in this picture. V-poles help us to stay straight, which can be a real help if your pony likes to jump to one side. They also help to keep us focused and encourage me to pick up my feet over the fence!

- build a showjumping course using just poles on the ground to develop your eye for seeing a stride
- keep fences small during training
- watch top riders and take note of what they do. You can then do exactly the same with your pony when you get home!

Half-hour RIDING HACKS!

30 min

FLATWORK

Follow my simple, speedy plan to supercharge your flatwork sessions!

Riding three ponies after school means I'm super busy and having a structure to follow when schooling helps to keep me and the ponies focused and our sessions productive. Check out my half-hour flatwork plan...

Starting out

10 min

I always spend the first five minutes of my warm-up session in walk – getting Rolo's muscles gradually ready for action. I include lots of halt transitions to check how responsive he is. As I progress to trot, I continue to ride plenty of transitions between and within paces. This is a great way to make sure he's listening to my aids!

Stepping up

10 min

Time to fine-tune our dressage skills as we prep for upcoming comps! Practising straight and accurate lines with poles gives our scores a big boost, so I spend time focusing on riding perfect lines – I mix it up between the centre line, along the three-quarter line and across the diagonals. Then, for the ultimate straightness test, I ride just off the track!

⏱ **5 min**

Next level

To keep Rolo flexible, I add shallow loops and different-sized circles on both reins. Rolo needs to bend through his ribcage, not just turn his neck, so I press with my inside leg and support him with my outside rein.

⏱ **5 min**

That's a wrap!

I always finish on a good note and then spend part of my cool-down period asking Rolo to stretch his head and neck down in trot. I then spend as long as I can walking him off to bring his heart rate back down slowly.

HEARD IT FROM HARLOW

It's important to not cut any corners when warming up and cooling down your pony, otherwise he might get injured! If you're short on time, set a timer on your phone for when to move on.

Why I LOVE Welshies

Welsh ponies hold a very special place in my heart

Picture perfect

You can't deny that Welsh ponies have the cutest faces in the world! Their dainty heads and small, pointed ears just make them sooo loveable and ideal models.

Awesome four

There are four types of Welsh pony, Section A, B, C and D. Each type has height and conformation requirements so they're easily recognisable. But it also means they come in all shapes and sizes.

Bubbly and brave

Welsh ponies have adorable personalities! They're cheeky, super-fun to hang out with and are often really bold, so they make the perfect pals for epic adventures!

Part of the crew

Part-bred Welshies, like Popcorn, are super-popular because they have all the fab qualities of Welsh ponies but with added extras! They even have their own breed register, but to be accepted, they have to have at least 12.5% pure Welsh blood.

Marvellous movements

Due to their small but striking build, Welsh ponies have amazing paces. They're mega flashy, so excel in the show ring, as well as many other disciplines!

THE LOWDOWN

Did you know that the Welsh breed originated in the mountains of Wales? In the olden days, they were originally used in coal mines but they turned out to be fab riding ponies, too!

POPCORN'S POINTERS

Pure and part-bred Welsh ponies like me will happily turn our hooves to anything! From dressage to driving and showing to showjumping, we have tons of talent!

Picture perfect

Check out my top tips for taking the best pony pics!

Find the right light

Make sure the lighting is even – for example, you don't want a tree behind to be really sunny and your pony to be in a dark spot. Try to find a spot with background and foreground in the same light. Avoid having harsh shadows or bright light, too, especially on your pony's face.

Have a helper

Grab a friend to help get your pony's attention, encourage him to look in the right direction and prick his ears forward. The trick? A tub of treats!

Play around with colours

You guys know I love a matchy set, but playing around with outfits and colours is so much fun! When it's sunny, vibrant colours really stand out, but neutral tones and cool shades look really great, too!

Take lots of shots

Get as many pics as possible so you have loads of options to choose from! Ponies like to fidget and look around, so getting tons of shots means you're sure to get the perfect snap!

Keep it real

Try to keep everything in proportion so it looks as real as possible. Avoid taking pics from crazy angles that will make your pony's legs look super-long or short!

Rolo is a showing pro – he loves to flick his toes and show off to the judge!

PONY

CROSSWORD CONUNDRUM!

DOWN
1 What was the discipline of my first comp with Panda?
2 What breed is Cloudy?
4 What colour is Popcorn?
5 What colour is Cloudy?
10 What month did Popcorn join the family?

ACROSS
3 What month was Popcorn born in?
6 What breed is Panda?
7 What is Rolo's best discipline?
8 What month was Panda born in?
9 What breed is Rolo?

PUZZLES

Fill in the crossword using the clues, then use the answers to complete the wordsearch!

WACKY WORDSEARCH!

M	S	H	E	T	L	A	N	D	T
A	B	G	K	K	T	C	K	C	O
R	D	P	G	C	A	O	M	R	S
C	A	R	A	Z	R	N	A	E	H
H	R	J	E	L	A	N	Y	A	O
K	T	P	U	S	O	E	E	M	W
G	M	U	M	N	S	M	Z	D	I
J	O	S	U	O	E	A	I	U	N
M	O	Q	H	Y	M	R	G	N	G
X	R	E	K	N	D	A	I	E	O

How did you get on? Visit bit.ly/PONY_PUZZLES to check your answers!

CLOUDY DOES...

HACKING

There's so much you can do out hacking with your pony and Cloudy and I have some great ideas

What's not to love about hacking out in the countryside on your fave pony? Whether it's a gentle stroll to have a catch-up with friends or a blast in the open to blow away the cobwebs, hacking is sooo much fun for ponies and their riders.

What is hacking?

Hacking simply means leaving the yard to go out for a ride, either along roads, lanes or bridlepaths.

What's involved?

You can choose to go out with your friends on their ponies or go alone if you want some quiet time. What's more, hacking can be tailored to any level rider, so if you feel the need for speed, why not have a gallop if it's safe to do so? If not, stick to walk instead.

When riding on the roads safety is the priority and you'll need to keep your concentration. You can ride side by side with a friend, but always go single file to let other road users pass easily. Talking of other road users, don't forget to say thank you if they slow down for you.

HEARD IT FROM HARLOW

If you're planning to go fast or jump some logs on your hack, make sure you've checked the ground on foot before you set off. That way, you can be sure it's safe to ride on and that there are no rabbit holes or other obstacles in the way.

CLOUDY'S CLUES

We ponies love nothing more than variety, so try venturing onto some new hacking routes whenever you can. Or, if you're planning a longer ride, why not pack a picnic and stop somewhere for lunch? Don't forget to pack a few treats for your pony and loosen his girth during your lunch break to give him a breather, too.

WHAT TO WEAR

There are a few essential items to wear out hacking, such as...

PONY

- a bridle that gives you full control ☐
- saddle – don't forget to check your girth! ☐
- boots if necessary ☐
- high-vis gear, especially on the roads ☐

RIDER

- correctly fitted hat that conforms to current safety standards ☐
- long-sleeved top to offer protection from brambles and sun ☐
- high-vis vest and bands ☐
- jods ☐
- long or short boots ☐
- gloves ☐
- fully charged phone in case of an emergency ☐

CLOUDY'S CLUES

Harlow and I absolutely love exploring, but she always lets a grown up at the yard know where we're going and roughly how long we're going to be. It's super important because, that way, if anything should happen to us, they'll know where to go to help us.

Perfect prep

There are lots of things you can do to make sure you stay safe out hacking, while making it fun for both you and your pony.

If you or your pony are newbies to hacking, it's a good idea to head out with a friend on a more experienced pony. On the road, you can

If you're planning to go fast, make sure you check the ground on foot first

tuck in on the inside, away from the traffic, so you both gain confidence from your friend.

There are lots of sights and sounds out hacking, so let your pony look at things, reassure him with a wither scratch and quietly ask him to go past. Singing to him will help him – and you – relax.

OUT AND ABOUT

Horsey days out are always so much fun!

I absolutely love going to horsey events, whether it's a huge competition like Burghley or a PONY mag Big Day Out, they're the next best thing to spending time with my own ponies. Find out my top four faves, right here!

1 Horse of the Year Show

I absolutely love watching all the amazing showing – it's definitely my fave part. The atmosphere is just incredible and there are so many stunning ponies!

2 PONY Big Day Out

Watching all the different acts and meeting my fans is so cool. I love signing things, too – I even signed a T-shirt with lipstick once – it was hilarious!

3 Burghley Horse Trials

Watching top eventers battle it out at such a gorgeous venue – the absolute dream day out! The shopping is pretty epic, too, and doing live Q&A sessions is so fun!

4 London International Horse Show

I looove the Christmassy vibes, as well as watching the Shetland Pony Grand National, of course! The Puissance is sooo cool, too – I can't believe how big the wall can get!

MAKE HORSEY CANDLE

Create a cute horsey candle in five easy steps!

Cosying up with a book, mug of hot chocolate and a candle is the ultimate chill-out vibe! And my adorable homemade horsey candle will add the perfect pony touch to this dreamy set up. Here's how to make it!

Let's go

Kit check

☐ 500ml glass jar
☐ LED tealight
☐ red, pink and orange tissue paper
☐ black card

1. Download the horse silhouette template from **bit.ly/HORSEY_CANDLE** and print onto black card. Ask an adult to help you cut around the horses.

2. Measure the height of your jar and divide it by three. Wrap a piece of string around your jar to measure the circumference.

3. On each piece of coloured tissue paper, draw a rectangle that's the same length as the circumference of your jar and a third of the depth.

4. Cut the three rectangles out and glue onto your jar, with the pink at the top, orange in the middle and yellow at the bottom. Then glue on the horsey silhouettes.

5. Once everything has dried in place, turn your candle on, pop it into the jar and enjoy the gorgeous glow of your horsey candle!

HEARD IT FROM HARLOW

You could change up the tissue paper colours so it's blue sky and lush grass, instead of a stunning sunset!

CARE guide:

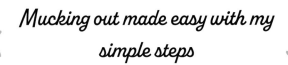
MUCKING OUT

Mucking out made easy with my simple steps

An essential part of pony care, mucking out is when you clean your pony's stable to give him a fresh bed to stand and sleep on, as well as water to drink and hay to munch on while he's inside. Here's how to muck out!

HEARD IT FROM HARLOW

If your pony is stabled at night, it's best to muck out in the morning and then skip out in the evening before putting him to bed – this is when you quickly only remove droppings and it helps to save on bedding!

Sweeping up to make it all neat and tidy!

1. First, you need to grab your wheelbarrow, shavings fork, shovel and a broom. Tie up your pony outside your stable with a haynet to munch on, or turn him out in the field. Then, take all your tools into his stable so you have them to hand.

2. Use your shavings fork to pick up the droppings, shaking it gently from side to side to allow clean bedding to drop back into the bed. Move all the clean bedding to the side and remove any wet bedding from the bottom of the bed.

3. Clear away any leftover hay and then use your broom to sweep up the floor. It's really helpful to use your shovel here, too, to pick up the loose, dirty bedding that you couldn't pick up with your fork earlier.

THE LOWDOWN

This is a guide to a full muck out, but there's another type called deep littering. This is when you remove the droppings each day, then the wet bedding once or twice a week. It can save bedding but isn't as good for your pony's breathing or hoof health.

4. If your pony's bed needs a top-up, clear a space at the side of his stable and ask an adult to bring a new bale. Open it into the cleared space and break it up with your fork. You'll probably need a new bale just once or twice a week!

5. Whether or not you've added fresh bedding, the next stage is to pull the bedding down from the sides. Use your fork to create a neat, flat bed in the middle and fluff it up at the sides to create banks – your pony will love his cosy bed!

6. Give your pony's stable a final sweep to make sure everything is neat and tidy. Then, empty his water bucket, give it a good scrub and refill it. Then put in some hay – after all that hard work, his stable is ready for him to come into!

Why I LOVE Shetlands

Shetland ponies are small but mighty, and oh so cute!

Speed demons

Shetland ponies are sooo speedy. I absolutely love doing zoomies with Cloudy and racing against our friends – plus, watching their fluff blow in the wind is adorable!

It's a small world

Shetlands are one of the smallest breeds in the world, which means they need all their gear in miniature form! Aren't tiny rugs, brushing boots and fly veils just the cutest thing ever?

Extra floofy!

Fluffy coats and crazy manes – two defining features every Shetland has! Cloudy's mane is impossible to tame, but I think he still looks awesome with his totally wild hair.

Cheeky chops

Shetlands are so well known for their ultra cheeky personalities! From escape artists to treat thieves, most Shetland ponies have habits and characteristics that make them a definite yard fave!

In good company

Due to their small size, big personalities and the fact they're good-doers, Shetland ponies make great companions for other horses. They also make amazing besties for humans, too – who doesn't love a cuddle and chat with a tiny, fluffy pony?

THE LOWDOWN

Did you know, Shetland ponies come from the Shetland Islands in Scotland? They were originally used in coal mines but today are really talented children's ponies!

CLOUDY'S CLUES

Shetland ponies like me don't require lots of hard feed. This is because my ancestors adapted to survive in rough conditions on little food – we're known to put weight on easily, too!

TRAILER
TOUR

Take a look around our amazing trailer, all set up for adventuring

My favourite thing about the trailer is being able to open up the sides so the ponies can see out of the window – they absolutely love munching on a haynet while enjoying the view! It's also great because we can take three ponies out at the same time – cue even more epic days out!

HEARD IT FROM HARLOW

The mirror is a tack locker essential

The design is sooo sleek

It's crazy how much kit we can fit in!

The ponies love having a nose out the windows!

Comfy bedding for the precious cargo on board!

The trailer is actually enormous!

FAN-TASTIC

Take my extra tricky quiz to find out if you're a mega fan!

1 **What's my middle name?**

----

2 **What date is my birthday?**

A 1st September ☐

B 2nd September ☐

C 1st October ☐

3 **What's the age difference between me and Harlen?**

----

4 **What's my fave subject at school?**

A Maths ☐

B Science ☐

C English ☐

5 **How old was Harlen when he first rode Popcorn?**

6 **Where did I go skiing with horses?**

A Austria ☐

B France ☐

C Switzerland ☐

7 Who did I have a jumping lesson with in Qatar?

8 What's the name of the model pony in my first Instagram post?

9 What accessory makes up my signature look on Star Stable?

A Heart sunglasses ☐

B Star saddlepad ☐

C Star sunglasses ☐

10 What's the name of the Shetland in my first horsey YouTube video?

A Teddy ☐

B Cloudy ☐

C Bear ☐

11 How many times did I fall off in my first bareback jumping session?

I scored ____ /12

Check your answers at bit.ly/HARLOW_FAN

12 What do I call Popcorn?

A Heart horse ☐

B Love horse ☐

C Happy horse ☐

I'm a...

0–4 points
Mini fan!
You might need to watch more of my YouTube videos!

5–9 points
Major fan!
You're a solid fan of the White family!

10–12 points
Mega fan!
You know me better than anyone else!

AWESOME AUTUMN

Freshly clipped coats and colourful backdrops – sure signs that autumn is upon us!

As the leaves turn from green to yellow to red, I can't resist getting some stunning autumnal pics with my ponies – especially when they look smart with their fab haircuts! One thing's for sure, autumn is absolutely gorgeous.

RIDING

Making a splash ☐

Rain is every equestrian's worst nightmare, but I don't let it stop me and my ponies! As the wetter weather approaches, the type of puddles that are perfect for water training start to appear and we love to make the most of them. Splashing through muddy puddles (after checking they're safe) is not only fun for the ponies, it's also a great way to boost their confidence with water.

Hard graft ☐

Practice makes perfect, right? And as the days get shorter, I spend more time riding in the school, which means I'm working hard with the ponies to improve all our skills. Whether it's brushing up on our jump-off technique or polishing off our centre lines, putting in the hours is sure to set us up for success!

CARE

Fresh trim ☐

That feeling when you run your hands over a freshly clipped coat – utter perfection. Autumn is the time of year when the ponies have their first haircuts. Clipping means I can continue riding throughout winter without the ponies getting too hot, and when I put them to bed in the evenings, I tuck them up in cosy rugs to keep them warm.

Getting prepped ☐

Organising my kit, checking the fields and preparing for the winter ahead is an essential autumn task! Before the weather takes a turn for the worse and we're covered head to toe in mud, I make sure the fields are in top-notch condition by poo picking, removing poisonous plants, securing fencing and checking water troughs.

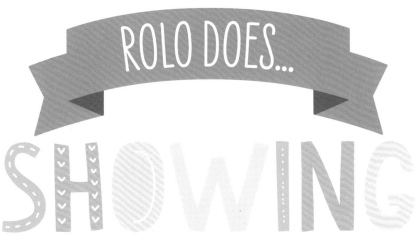

ROLO DOES...
SHOWING

Thinking of trying out showing this season? Rolo, the showing superstar, is here to help

I'm so lucky to have ponies who do well in different disciplines, and Rolo's biggest talent shines through in the show ring. Did you know there are hundreds of showing classes for ponies? From mountain and moorlands to working hunters, there's a class for everyone.

What is showing?

In simple terms, showing is the judge's opinion on which pony best fits the criteria of the class he's entered into. You may be awarded marks for different things, such as your pony's conformation, type and manners.

What's involved?

Depending on the class, you'll usually be asked to walk, trot and sometimes canter around the ring with the other ponies who are competing. Then you'll line up to do an individual show in front of the judge. They might even ask you to remove your pony's saddle to trot him up in-hand. After that, all the riders go around the ring again and the final placings are decided. If you hear your number called, you'll need to line up with the other winners.

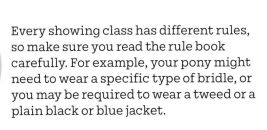

HEARD IT FROM HARLOW

Every showing class has different rules, so make sure you read the rule book carefully. For example, your pony might need to wear a specific type of bridle, or you may be required to wear a tweed or a plain black or blue jacket.

Rolo's round-up

Some showing classes require ponies to be plaited and others don't. I take part in mountain and moorland classes, which means I must be shown unplaited. And because I'm a Dartmoor, I compete in the small-breed classes, alongside Exmoors, Shetlands and Welsh Mountain ponies – cool, huh?

WHAT TO WEAR

The rules on dress vary depending on your class, but generally you'll need...

PONY

- bridle with anappropriate bit, noseband and browband for that class ☐
- straight-cut saddle ☐
- discreet, plain-coloured numnah ☐

RIDER

- hat – the colour and style depends on the class ☐
- hairnet and bow to keep hair neat and tidy ☐
- shirt and tie ☐
- tweed, navy or black jacket ☐
- beige or canary jods ☐
- short boots ☐
- gloves ☐

Rolo's round-up

Brown tack is more correct for showing – I have a straight-cut saddle, as it shows off my movement better. The style of bridle depends on what class you're entering, but make sure you choose one that complements your pony's head to show him off as best you can.

Perfect prep

Show ponies need to be well mannered, well schooled and able to stand still while the judge inspects them.

You'll need to teach your pony to be calm and obedient while walking, trotting and cantering around the ring with other ponies, so work on this at home before you

> *At smaller shows you'll often come across fun classes such as pony with the longest tail*

enter a class. And don't forget you'll need to perform a short individual show that includes walk, trot and canter on both reins, before your final halt in front of the judge.

Finally, teach your pony to trot up in-hand and make sure he's used to being handled so the judge can inspect him safely and easily!

"Panda gives me so much confidence and puts his all into every activity!"

DAY IN
THE LIFE

Find out what Popcorn, Cloudy, Rolo and Panda get up to each day!

My weekends are super-busy with four ponies to ride, and we often take them out to competitions or arena hire, which requires lots of preparation! Here's what a typical home Saturday looks like for me and my fave boys!

7am
Time for breakfast and a rug change for the day ahead!

7.30am
Once the ponies' bowls are licked clean, they're turned out so they can spend time grazing and playing!

Brothers having fun together!

11am
I bring Cloudy in from the field, give him a thorough groom and then go for a hack with my friends on their Shetlands – we obviously go zoomies around the fields!

12pm
Cloudy goes back into the field and I grab myself some lunch – I need lots of energy for my jam-packed afternoon!

If Popcorn is in the field when we arrive at the yard, he always neighs and runs over to the gate when he sees our car – it's the cutest thing ever!!!

1pm

Popcorn is usually waiting for me at his field gate, so I bring him in and get him ready for a schooling session. I like to mix up the ponies' exercise routines because it keeps them happy, plus it's more fun for me!

2.30pm

I like to end my session with Popcorn by walking him off around the fields, which he loves! I then wash him off and put him back in his stable before bringing Rolo in to give him a quick jump!

4.30pm

Rolo was epic but even though I've ridden three ponies, the day hasn't finished just yet! I bring Panda in from the field – it's his day off today, so he's been chilling.

5pm

I give the boys their dinners, then it's time to top up water buckets, make night-time haynets and skip out the stables. I rug up Popcorn and Panda, but Rolo needs a bath before bed as we're off to a show tomorrow!

6pm

Rolo is finally sparking clean and ready for bed. With Mum's help, I pack the horsebox to save us time in the morning, as it's an early start! I give the ponies a quick cuddle and check them over before heading home for dinner and then it's off to bed!

Half-hour RIDING HACKS!

30 min

JUMPING

Get the most out of your short jumping sessions with these handy exercises!

I don't always have time to set up a full course of jumps or a fancy grid, but that doesn't stop me from improving my jumping skills! Here's my plan for a quick and effective jump sesh...

10 min

Starting out

Like in my flatwork sessions, I spend the first five minutes of my jumping warm-up in walk – making sure Rolo is working actively and is supple by riding lots of turns and circles. I do the same in trot and then, when I ask for canter, I use the whole of the arena to practise shortening and lengthening his stride. This helps to wake up his muscles and get him thinking forwards!

10 min

Stepping up

Instead of setting up lots of jumps, I place 10 poles on the floor around the arena, all in random places so I can pretend I'm riding a course! This helps me focus on getting the perfect rhythm and riding really good approaches. Even though I'm not jumping yet, Rolo still has to think carefully about where he's putting his feet, so it definitely gets him in the zone, too.

⏱ **5 min**

Next level

I like to set up a fence at X because I can ride it in so many different ways. After popping it a couple of times on each rein, thinking about a straight approach, I practise jumping on an angle and while riding a circle – tricky, but so good for our training!

⏱ **5 min**

That's a wrap!

When I'm happy with how Rolo has jumped, I spend two minutes of my cool-down trotting large around the arena. This allows Rolo to stretch and slowly reduce his heart rate. I then walk him on a long rein for as long as I can before giving him a big pat!

HEARD IT FROM HARLOW

I put boots on my ponies when jumping or doing fast work to protect them. To keep myself safe, I always wear my body protector when jumping bigger or riding challenging exercises, too.

HEARD IT FROM HARLOW

Make sure the sound throughout your video is even and there aren't any really loud bits! You can also add transitions and text to give it an extra-professional finish.

At the movies

You'll make the most amazing videos with my tips!

Make it interesting

It's a good idea to have a rough plan of what you want your video to look like. Maybe your lesson or competition round is the highlight, but including an intro and things that go on before and after the main event is key to an amazing video!

Film everything

Try to film as much as you can to keep it natural. You could even leave your camera on a tripod while it's running to see if anything funny or crazy happens – that's sure to give you some great content! If you only film the things you want, it does make editing much quicker but you can easily cut your videos to make them a lot snappier.

Use editing apps

If you don't have a camera, you can film on your phone and download a video-editing app to put it together – there are loads, so try a few to see which one you like the most!

Time it wisely

How long your video is depends on whether you're putting it on YouTube or Instagram – but, as a rule, avoid making them too long, otherwise they can be boring! My YouTube videos are always around half an hour long – but sometimes they're slightly longer if it's been a full-on day!

Match your music

You might need to spend time looking for the right music, as it has to match the vibe! I save videos I've seen that have cool music, and that really speeds up the editing process!

MAKE CRUNCHY HORSESHOES

Follow my simple step-by-step to make these super- yummy snacks!

I f you're going for a sleepover with friends, organising a pony picnic, having a bake sale for charity, or just fancy a tasty afternoon snack, these crunchy horseshoes are just what you need in your life! Here's how to make them...

Let's go

Kit check

To make six crunchy horseshoes, you'll need...
- ☐ 200g milk or dark chocolate
- ☐ 80g cornflakes
- ☐ 36 white chocolate chunks or drops

1 Break up your chocolate into small pieces and ask an adult to help you melt them in a heatproof bowl over a pan of boiling water.

2 Weigh out your cornflakes into a bowl and pour in the melted chocolate. Mix it all together until the cornflakes are well covered.

3 Line a tray with greaseproof paper and divide the mixture into six. Space each one out on the tray.

4 Time for the messy bit! Use your hands to mould the chocolatey cornflakes into horseshoe shapes and then add three white chocolate chunks on each side to resemble the nails.

5 Place the tray in the fridge and leave to set. Once they're set, you can tuck into these delicious snacks!

HEARD IT FROM HARLOW

If you're struggling to mould the mixture into horseshoes with your hands, you could use a horseshoe-shaped cutter and spoon the mixture into it.

Meet ROLO

FACT FILE

- **DATE OF BIRTH**
  18 April 2014
- **HEIGHT**
  12hh
- **BREED**
  Dartmoor
- **BEST EQUINE FRIEND**
  Popcorn
- **FAVE TREAT**
  Stud Muffins!
- **FAVE ACTIVITY**
  Jumping
- **BEST COLOUR**
  Purple

Rolo's the pony who introduced me to the wonderful world of showing and really helped me to kickstart my showing journey.

He has the most gorgeous paces and really flicks his toes when showing off to the judges. But behind all the glitz and glamour is a crazy pony who loooves his food and is the messiest eater ever! He also loves to pick up his feed bowl with his teeth and throw it around his stable – it's definitely his funniest habit!

Sweet like chocolate

Rolo has such a sweet personality and loves his brothers sooo much! Whenever I take someone else out to ride, he always calls after them – his neigh is super-high pitched, but so cute!

Even though he's an actual speed demon when it comes to showjumping, he always takes care of me. Plus, we get the most adorable jumping pics because he always looks so happy with his ears pricked, and he tucks his knees up so nicely, too!

Insider info

Rolo literally has the most perfect teeth! They are sooo white and so clean, they honestly don't look real!

He has the most gorgeous paces and really flicks his toes

HEARD IT FROM HARLOW

Competing at Horse of the Year Show with Rolo is my ultimate goal! The atmosphere there is really incredible and I'd love to be able to say I've ridden in the famous HOYS arena!

Why I LOVE Connies

Connemaras are absolute characters and sooo gorgeous!

Gorgeous greys

Connies come in lots of different colours, but the most common is grey. Panda is super white, so he looks fantastic when he's clean, but it certainly takes a lot of work to get him sparkling!

Very versatile

It's safe to say that Connemaras are incredibly talented and amazing at so many disciplines. From eventing to showing – they can do it all!

Big hearts

Connemaras are known for having lovely temperaments. They have kind hearts, are super-cuddly and very intelligent! Connies are caring, too, which makes them ideal children's ponies.

Hey, good lookin'

I can't get over how stunning Panda's face is! Like most Connies, he has a cute head, bright eyes and neat, pointy ears. His mane is sooo soft and silky, too!

Best of both worlds

The average size of a Connie is 14–14.2hh, so they can be ridden by children and adults. Panda is big enough for my mum to ride, so she can finally get back into riding properly! This means we can go adventuring together – it's sooo exciting!

THE LOWDOWN

Connemaras are native to Ireland – they originally came from the west coast where the landscape is beautiful but rugged. That is why they're well-adapted to living in harsh conditions!

PANDA'S PROPOSAL

Connemaras like me are perfect for children who are thinking of moving onto horses! Connies are considered a large pony breed, so we're the ideal in-between stage.

POPCORN DOES...
CROSS-COUNTRY

Cross-country is Popcorn's fave thing to do, so let's find out more about this fast and furious discipline

I don't know about you, but I think there's nothing more exciting than the thrill of jumping cross-country fences at speed!

If you've never tried it, why not give it a go this year? You can hire a course and take your own pony, or book a lesson at your local riding school.

What is cross-country?

Cross-country is one of the three phases of eventing and the most exciting one for many ponies and their riders, including me and Popcorn!

What's involved?

Courses are made up of different types of fences, such as drops, ditches, skinnies, arrowheads and water jumps. To do well, you'll need to jump clear without any run-outs or refusals, while also avoiding time faults.

Most courses have an optimum time, and you'll be penalised for every second over this time, as well as being more than 15 seconds too fast. To help them go at the right speed, some riders wear stopwatches so they know if they need to speed up or slow down – how cool is that?

It's important to walk the course in advance. You can usually do it the day before or on the morning if there's time. Each fence has a red flag on the right and a white one on the left, so make sure you jump them in the right direction!

POPCORN'S POINTERS

Did you know that cross-country is the ultimate test of trust and relationship between pony and rider? My job is to clear the fences and keep Harlow safe, and Harlow's job is to make sure I stay in a steady rhythm and balance and approach fences on a good line. We make a great team because we know each other so well!

WHAT TO WEAR

The great thing about cross-country is you can ride in your fave colours. Here's what to wear...

PONY
- bridle with a bit or noseband that gives you enough control ☐
- jumping saddle with stirrups and a secure girth ☐
- saddle pad ☐
- boots to protect legs ☐

RIDER
- correctly fitted skull cap and body protector ☐
- long-sleeved top in the colour of your choice ☐
- jodhpurs ☐
- long boots or short boots and gaiters ☐
- gloves ☐

POPCORN'S POINTERS

We ponies need to be in a good rhythm to jump clear. Practise staying in a cross-country canter out hacking to get your pony ready for the challenge ahead! It also helps if you can ride with a light seat in between the fences on a cross-country course. This takes the weight off his back and allows him to move more freely.

Perfect prep

With sooo many challenges along the way, it's important to do your homework. The best thing for brushing up on your cross-country skills is to hire a course and go with an instructor to help you.

Spend time researching courses near you to find one

Some riders wear stopwatches so they know if they need to speed up or slow down

POPCORN'S POINTERS

Did you know that a rustic fence – like the one I'm jumping on the far left – looks a lot like an XC fence to a pony? So, if you can't get out onto an actual cross-country course to practise, you can improvise in the arena! Cooooool!

with all the different fences you'll meet on course in a real competition. That way, you and your pony are sure to feel super-confident on the day of the event!

Your instructor can also teach you how to ride all the types of fences, and how to link them together, too.

There's nothing better than zoomies after school!

CARE guide: TACK CLEANING

Make your tack sparkle with my great guide

Looking after your fave pony's tack is an important task because it will keep it in tip-top condition, which means it'll last longer! Follow my six simple steps to perfectly clean tack.

Giving the bit a good clean and check over!

1. For the ultimate tack-cleaning session, you'll need a bucket of warm water, two sponges or cloths, leather soap and conditioner or leather balm. If your pony's tack is synthetic, you'll only need water and a sponge to clean it!

2. To get started, take apart the bridle piece by piece. Laying each part out on a towel in its correct position is really helpful here to keep it all in the right place! Then, remove your girth, stirrups and leathers from the saddle.

3. Use a damp sponge to clean the dirt off each part of your tack. Then pop your pony's bit and stirrups into the bucket of clean water and let them soak for a little while. Once clean, dry the bit and stirrups with a towel or cloth.

4. Grab your soap and pop some onto a clean sponge. Cleaning one piece at a time, work it into the leather to remove any stubborn dirt. Remember to skip this step and the next one if your tack is synthetic!

5. Leather conditioner or balm are used to care for and soften leather. It's an essential part of my tack-cleaning kit but I only condition my tack a couple of times a month – but sometimes more often if I've been riding in the rain!

6. Now it's the tricky part – putting it all back together! There are lots of parts to the bridle so ask for help if you need it – you don't want a wonky bridle! Then pop a cover on your saddle and put your bridle in a bag to keep them clean!

Pick of the

Find out which of my ponies you're most like with this amazing quiz!

1 What's your favourite colour?

Baby blue 4 points ☐

Green 2 points ☐

Purple 3 points ☐

Orange 5 points ☐

2 What's your favourite discipline?

Showing 3 points ☐

Cross-country 5 points ☐

Dressage 4 points ☐

Showjumping 2 points ☐

3 What's your favourite pace?

Walk 2 points ☐

Trot 1 point ☐

Canter 2 points ☐

Gallop 1 point ☐

4 What hair style do you prefer?

Curly and crazy 2 points ☐

Short and neat 5 points ☐

Long and flowing 3 points ☐

Cute and fluffy 4 points ☐

bunch

5 What's your favourite pony colour?

Palomino 5 points ☐

Cream dun 2 points ☐

Grey 4 points ☐

Brown 3 points ☐

6 Which breed is your fave?

Connemara 4 points ☐

Welsh pony 5 points ☐

Dartmoor 3 points ☐

Shetland 2 points ☐

7. What kind of friend are you?

Caring 1 point ☐

Funny 2 points ☐

Reliable 2 points ☐

Cheeky 1 point ☐

8. What's your fave kind of holiday?

Full of sports and adventures 1 point ☐

Relaxing, with plenty of pamper sessions 2 points ☐

Camping and jam-packed with activities 1 point ☐

Sight-seeing and travelling to different places 2 points ☐

9. What's your favourite season?

Spring 2 points ☐

Summer 2 points ☐

Autumn 1 point ☐

Winter 1 point ☐

10. What's your favourite snack?

Popcorn 5 points ☐

Candy floss 2 points ☐

Chocolate 3 points ☐

Crisps 4 points ☐

11. Which emoji do you love the most?

🐼 4 points ☐

🍿 5 points ☐

🍫 3 points ☐

☁️ 2 points ☐

I SCORED ___ POINTS!

How did you get on?

Add up the points to reveal which pony you're most like!

20–26 points
Cloudy
Your personality is a great fit with my Cloudy boy!

27–33 points
Rolo
You and Rolo would defo be BFFs in real life!

34–40 points
Panda
Panda is your perfect match!

41–48 points
Popcorn
You share loads with my heart horse, Popcorn!!

---

12 What does your dream hack involve?

A sunset beach ride 5 points ☐

Zoomies in the field 2 points ☐

Exploring new places 3 points ☐

Perfecting dressage moves 4 points ☐

WONDERFUL WINTER

Winter isn't so bad when the sun shines down and makes the frost sparkle!

RIDING

CARE

Frosty morning rides and snuggling up with the ponies to keep warm... winter isn't all doom and gloom! The ponies might get less time in the field, but that doesn't mean we have to stop having fun!

Lessons learnt ☐

Winter is the ideal time to try something new, whether or not you have your own pony! It could be a new discipline, dressage move or jumping exercise – either way, it's so much fun and, if it's with your pony, he'll appreciate the exciting new addition to his exercise routine!

Supple up ☐

Lots of ponies are turned out less over winter because of the field conditions. This means they don't get the natural exercise they're used to, so can become a little stiff from standing in their stables. I like to spend time doing lots of in-hand stretches with Popcorn, Cloudy and Rolo to help keep them supple – they also love the extra treats they get as a reward for doing a fab job!

Forage fiesta ☐

Grass doesn't grow as much during winter so the ponies eat more hay and hard feed to make sure their diets are fully balanced and to help them maintain condition. Popcorn, Cloudy and Rolo don't need much more feed because they're good-doers but having an extra bit of hay at night helps them to stay warm when the temp drops.

Checked out ☐

All my ponies have a visit from the vet and an annual health check in winter to ensure they're in good health and condition. It's an important date in the ponies' diaries and gives me the chance to speak to my vet about any worries and get lots of advice. Once they've had their heart, lungs, teeth, eyes and body condition checked, I know they're ready for all the adventures coming our way!

WINTER

All the photoshoot outfits!

Maybe not Popcorn's best angle!

BEHIND THE SCENES

My fave memories from making my 2024 yearbook!

HEARD IT
FROM
HARLOW

*Dreamy scenes
at the farm*

HEARD IT
FROM
HARLOW

*Post-shoot
pack up!*

Zoomies with Cloudy boy

Cheeky Panda!

All hands on deck

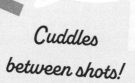

HEARD IT FROM HARLOW

Cuddles between shots!

Sleepy boy!

HEARD IT FROM HARLOW

Scratchies for my superstar!

That's the spot!

Getting Rolo ready for action